NAPE

BACK

RUMP

TAIL

ROGER TORY PETERSON'S
ABC OF BIRDS

A Book for Little Birdwatchers

Text by Linda Westervelt

Illustration by Roger Tory Peterson • Photography by Roger Tory Peterson and Seymour Levin

Design by Rudy Hoglund

is for Albatross.

Like a glider plane, the albatross glides.

On the winds of the ocean, the albatross rides.

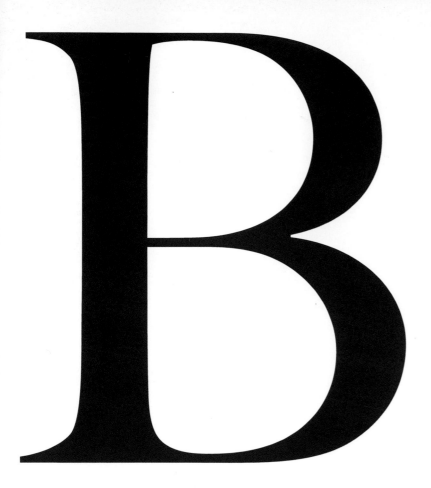

is for Blackbird.

Dark like the night, blackbirds shine in the light,
and some are dressed in the colors of the sun.

is for Cardinal.

The beautiful cardinal is a pretty brown or brilliant red and wears a crest upon its head.

D

is for Duck.

Cute puddle ducks, diving ducks, and
a duck with a spiky tail feather—"quack-
quack," "whoo-eek," "prrip-prrip"—
ducks pictured all together.

E

is for Egret.

Like a snowflake ballerina in *The Nutcracker* ballet, the beautiful egret flies away.

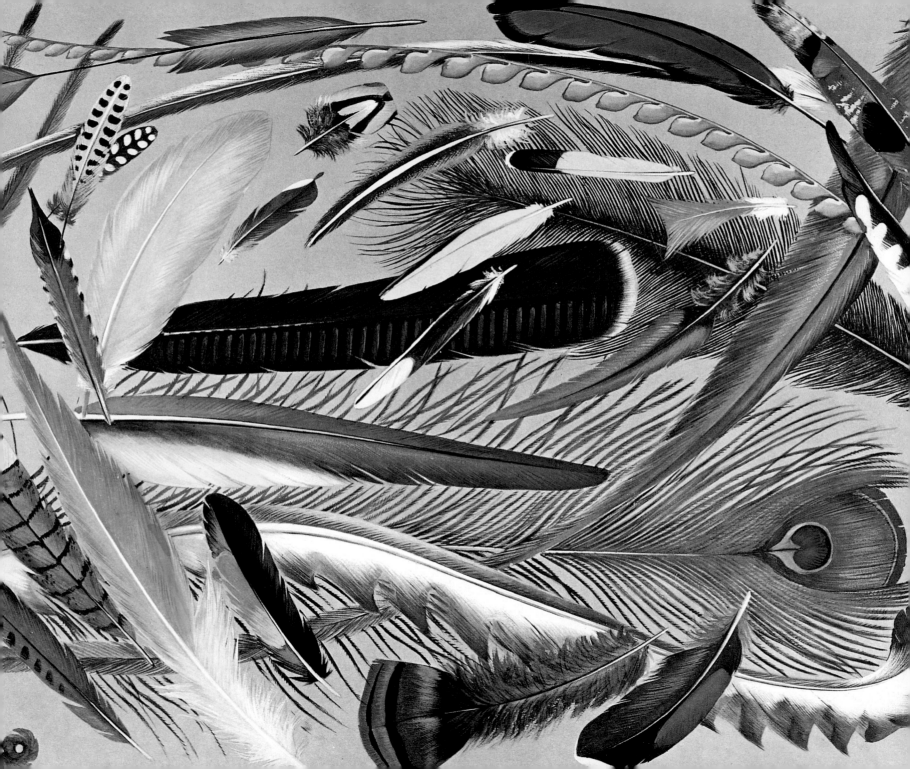

F

is for Feathers and Feet.

Birds of a foot flocked together.

Only a bird can grow a feather.

G

is for Gull.

Sailing on a sea breeze, the gull looks
for fish, popcorn, a chicken wing—
gulls eat almost everything.

H is for Hummingbird.

Like helicopters, hummingbirds fly up, down, backward, forward, side-to-side, and even upside down.

I is for Ibis.

Meet the beautiful ibis,
Scarlet—flaming red,
a bright zoo starlet.

J is for Jay.

Jays are green. Jays are blu
Jays are curious—
noisy too!

K is for Kingfisher.

Kingfishers fish every day
perched on branches above a bay.

L is for Loon.

Diving, swimming, laughing loon,
cries and screams at night in June.

M

is for Meadowlark.

In spring by a meadow,
a lovely meadowlark
perches on a post
and sings "spring o' the year."

N

is for Nest.

On branches,
in logs, on
roofs and
cliff faces—
birds build
their nests
in dozens
of places.

O

is for Owl.

In the night, sharp eyes
and ears watch and listen.
"Whoo, whoo, whoo."

P is for Pelican.

The pelican's pouch scoops up fish like a net—catfish, crayfish, chubs, and mullet.

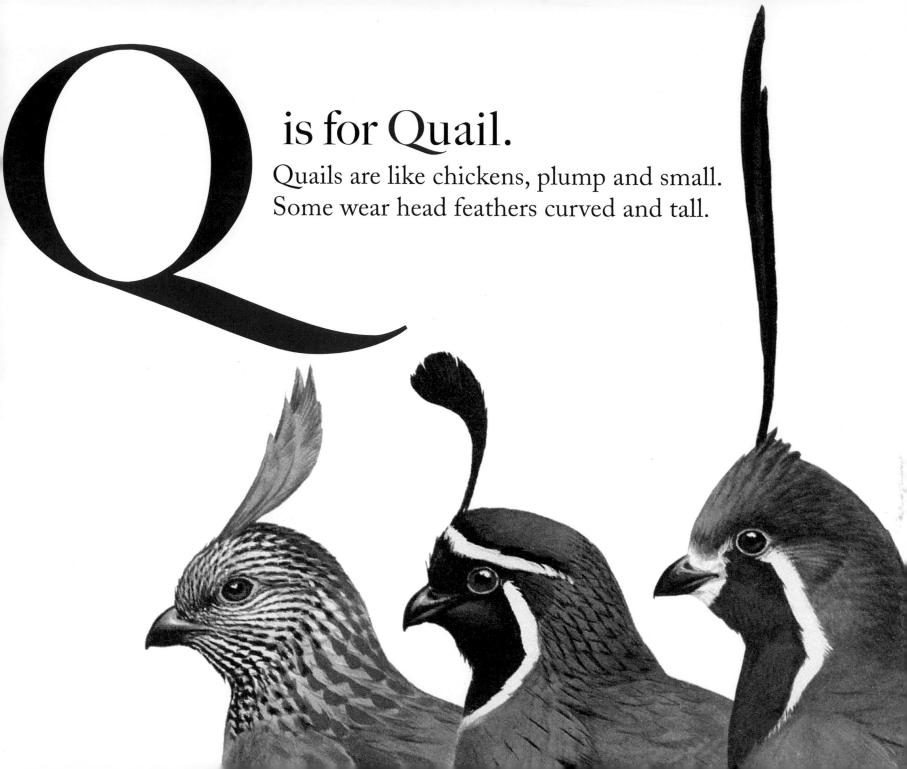

Q is for Quail.

Quails are like chickens, plump and small.
Some wear head feathers curved and tall.

R

is for Roadrunner.

"Coo-coo-coo-coo-coo-coo."
The roadrunner is a cuckoo that runs.

S is for Spoonbill.

Spoonbills live on marshes and lagoons. Their long flat bills are shaped like spoons.

T is for Tail.

Tails steer and lift a bird's weight. When fanned, like a peacock, they attract a new mate.

U is for Umbrella Bird.

The Umbrella Bird wears a black umbrella upon its head, and a neck like a balloon of a rosy red.

V is for Vulture.

Vultures are like eagles—in circles they fly.
They have small bald heads and a very sharp eye.

W

is for Woodpecker.

"Knock, knock, knock,"
the big woodpecker knocks.
All woodpeckers knock on wood.

X

is for Xantus'
Murrelet.

Like penguins, murrelets
swim and fish in
the seas.

They travel
in pairs or with
their families.

Y

is for
Yellow-Throated
Warbler.

Creeping along a branch,
this yellow-throated shopper
picks up a caterpillar, an ant,
or a grasshopper.

Z

is for Zenaida Dove.

Once upon a time, a prince named this sweet dove Zenaida after the princess he loved.

Guide to Illustrations

These captions include the following information: Species, medium, publication for which the artwork was created or most recently revised, and year of execution or publication. The locations of photographs are identified; those taken by Seymour Levin are noted as such. For resources, see page 31. For copyright information, see page 32.

Cover
Keel-Billed Toucan
Mixed media, *A Field Guide to Mexican Birds,* 1973

Back Cover
Clockwise (from the large penguin at right): King, Little Blue, Chinstrap, Erect-Crested, Adélie, Gentoo, Royal, Galápagos, and Peruvian penguins
Mixed media, *Penguins,* 1979

Title Page
American Flamingo, Brownsville, Texas
Photograph by Seymour Levin, 1993

A is for Albatross
Gray-Headed Albatross
South Georgia Island, Antarctica
Photograph, *Penguins,* 1979

B is for Blackbird
TOP ROW (ALL LEFT TO RIGHT): Giant Cowbird*, Melodious Blackbird*, Yellow-Headed Blackbird†, Red-Winged Blackbird†

MIDDLE ROW: Chestnut-Headed Oropendola*, Yellow-Billed Cacique*, Great-Tailed Grackle† (male), Great-Tailed Grackle† (female)
BOTTOM ROW: Montezuma Oropendola*, Yellow-Winged Cacique* (male), Yellow-Winged Cacique* (female)
BIRDS WITH ASTERISK (*): Mixed media, *A Field Guide to Mexican Birds,* 1973
BIRDS WITH CROSS (†): Mixed media, *A Field Guide to Western Birds,* 1990

C is for Cardinal
Northern Cardinals with Rosa Multiflora, male in foreground, female at rear
Mixed media, limited-edition Mill Pond Press print, 1973

D is for Duck
CLOCKWISE FROM UPPER LEFT: Northern Pintails, Northern Shovelers, Barrow's Goldeneyes, Cinnamon Teal, Hooded Merganser, Canvasbacks, Ruddy Duck, Mallards, Lesser Scaups, Wood Ducks, Blue-Winged Teals, Buffleheads
NOTE: With ducks pictured in pairs, the bird in the foreground is the male of the species, while the bird at rear is female.
Mixed media, *A Field Guide to the Birds (Eastern North America),* revised 1996

E is for Egret
Great Egret
J. N. "Ding" Darling Refuge, Sanibel, Florida
Photograph by Seymour Levin, 1992

F is for Feathers and Feet
Mixed media, *The World of Birds,* 1964

G is for Gull
Laughing Gull, winter plumage
Padre Island, Texas
Photograph by Seymour Levin, 1993

H is for Hummingbird
CLOCKWISE FROM UPPER LEFT: Mexican Sheartail, Garnet-Throated Hummingbird, Rufous-Crested Coquette, Violet Sabrewing, Magnificent (Rivoli's) Hummingbird, Bumblebee Hummingbird, Sparkling-Tailed (Dupont's) Hummingbird, Stripe-Tailed Hummingbird (female), Stripe-Tailed Hummingbird (male), Black-Crested Coquette, Black-Fronted Hummingbird, White-Eared Hummingbird, Plain-Capped Starthroat (behind H), Long-Tailed Hermit
Mixed media, *A Field Guide to Mexican Birds,* 1973

I is for Ibis
Scarlet Ibis, Busch Gardens, Tampa, Florida
Photograph by Seymour Levin, 1994

J is for Jay
Green Jay, mixed media, *A Field Guide to Mexican Birds,* 1973

K is for Kingfisher
Belted Kingfishers, male in foreground
Mixed media, *A Field Guide to the Birds (Eastern North America),* revised 1996

L IS FOR LOON
Common Loon, summer plumage in
foreground, winter plumage at rear
Mixed media, *A Field Guide to the Birds
(Eastern North America)*, revised 1996

M IS FOR MEADOWLARK
Eastern Meadowlark
Nicoria, Florida
Photograph by Seymour Levin, 1993

N IS FOR NEST
European Goldfinch
Mixed media, *The World of Birds*, 1964

O IS FOR OWL
TOP ROW (ALL LEFT TO RIGHT): Striped
Owl, Spectacled Owl, Stygian Owl
MIDDLE ROW: Elf Owl, Mottled Owl
BOTTOM ROW: Crested Owl, Least Pygmy-
Owl, Black-and-White Owl, Ferruginous
Pygmy-Owl, Unspotted Saw-Whet Owl
Mixed media, *A Field Guide to Mexican
Birds*, 1973

P IS FOR PELICAN
Eurasian White Pelican
Lake Nakuru, Kenya
Photograph, 1993

Q IS FOR QUAIL
LEFT TO RIGHT: Elegant Quail, Gambel's
Quail, Mountain Quail
Mixed media, *A Field Guide to Mexican
Birds*, 1973

R IS FOR ROADRUNNER
Greater Roadrunner
Mixed media, limited-edition Mill Pond
Press print, 1976

S IS FOR SPOONBILL
Roseate Spoonbill, Rabbit Island, Texas
Photograph by Seymour Levin, 1993

T IS FOR TAIL
LEFT: Common Peacock
India, photograph, 1980
UPPER RIGHT: Resplendent Quetzal
Mixed media, *A Field Guide to Mexican
Birds*, 1973
LOWER RIGHT: Nightingale Wren
Mixed media, *A Field Guide to Mexican
Birds*, 1973

U IS FOR UMBRELLA BIRD
Umbrella Bird
Mixed media, *The World of Birds*, 1964

V IS FOR VULTURE
King Vulture
Mixed media, *The World of Birds*, 1964

W IS FOR WOODPECKER
Pileated Woodpecker
J. N. "Ding" Darling Refuge, Sanibel, Florida
Photograph by Seymour Levin, 1994

X IS FOR XANTUS' MURRELET
Xantus' Murrelet, mixed media, *A Field
Guide to Western Birds*, 1990

Y IS FOR YELLOW-THROATED WARBLER
Yellow-Throated Warbler
Mixed media, *A Field Guide to Western
Birds*, 1990

Z IS FOR ZENAIDA DOVE
Zenaida Dove
Mixed media, *A Field Guide to Mexican
Birds*, 1973

RESOURCES

*A Field Guide to the Birds (Eastern North
America)*. Boston: Houghton Mifflin, 1934
(revised 1939, 1941, 1947, 1980, 1996).

A Field Guide to Western Birds. Boston: Houghton
Mifflin, 1941 (revised 1961, 1990).

The World of Birds (with James Fisher).
New York: Doubleday, 1964.

A Field Guide to the Birds of Mexico (with
Edward Chalif). Boston: Houghton Mifflin, 1973.

Penguins. Boston: Houghton Mifflin, 1979.

The following artwork appears courtesy of
Mill Pond Press, Inc., Venice, Florida 34292:
Cardinal, Owl, Roadrunner, and Quail.

For Ashley Peterson,
Owen Henry,
and Olivia Henry,
with love.

First published in the United States of America in 1995 by
UNIVERSE PUBLISHING
A Division of Rizzoli International Publications, Inc.
300 Park Avenue South
New York, NY 10010

Text © 1995 Linda Westervelt
Some photographs © Seymour Levin
Some photographs © Roger Tory Peterson
Illustration © Roger Tory Peterson
For copyright dates and artist information for individual pictures, see pages 30–31
Cardinal, Owl, Quail, and Roadrunner images appear courtesy of
Mill Pond Press, Venice, Florida 34292

95 96 97 98 99 / 10 9 8 7 6 5 4 3 2 1

Printed in Hong Kong

Library of Congress Cataloging-in-Publication Data

Peterson, Roger Tory, 1908–
  [ABC of birds]
  Roger Tory Peterson's ABC of birds: a book for little birdwatchers
text by Linda Westervelt; illustration and photography by Roger Tory Peterson;
photography by Seymour Levin; design by Rudy Hoglund.
    p.   cm.
Summary: Photographs, paintings, and simple text present different birds and
some avian features for each letter of the alphabet.
  ISBN 0–7893–0009–5 (alk. paper)
  1. Birds—Juvenile literature. 2. English language—Alphabet—Juvenile literature.
[1. Birds. 2. Alphabet.] I. Westervelt, Linda. II. Levin, Seymour, ill. III.
Hoglund, Rudy, des. IV. Title.
QL676.2.P465 1995
598—dc20   95–15540
CIP   AC

CROWN————————————————

BEAK————————————————

CHIN————————————

BREAST————————

BELLY————————

WING————————